#16
Donald Bruce Kaufman
Brentwood Branch
11820 San Vicente Blvd.
Los Angeles, CA 60049

W9-BHA-564

Shelve
downstairs

The Library of Cells™

Cell Functions

Understanding How Cells Work

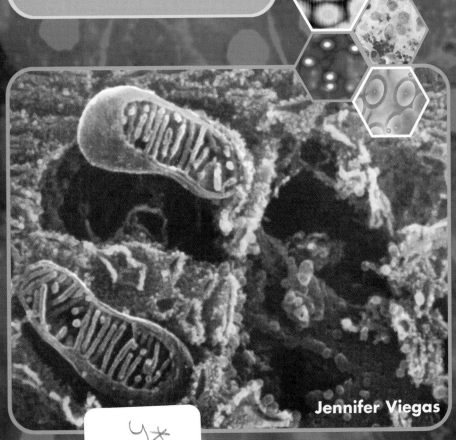

Jennifer Viegas

The Rosen Publishing Group, Inc., New York

Published in 2005 by The Rosen Publishing Group, Inc.
29 East 21st Street, New York, New York 10010

Library of Congress Cataloging-in-Publication

Viegas, Jennifer.
Cell functions: understanding how cells work/by Jennifer
Viegas.—1st ed.
    p. cm.—(The library of cells)
Includes bibliographical references and index.
ISBN 1-4042-0320-6 (library binding)
1. Cells—Juvenile literature. I. Title. II. Series.
QH582.5.V54 2005
571.6—dc22

2004016704

Manufactured in the United States of America

On the cover: This colored scanning electron micrograph
of a human pancreatic cell shows mitochondria, colored
blue, and the network of folded membranes and ribosomes
called the rough endoplasmic reticulum, colored yellow.

Contents

Chapter One   Life, Catalyst, Action!   4

Chapter Two   Protein Builders   12

Chapter Three   Cell Processes and Movement   21

Chapter Four   Mini Power Stations   27

Chapter Five   Specialized Cells   36

                   Glossary   42

                   For More Information   45

                   For Further Reading   46

                   Bibliography   46

                   Index   47

Chapter One

Life, Catalyst, Action!

A movie about the cells in your body would have to be an action film. Cells are always busy. Even when you are at rest or sleeping, some form of activity is taking place in your body's cells—all 10 trillion of them. They are all working on your behalf, to keep you breathing, energized, fed, and alive.

Cells themselves are living structures. They are the smallest units of life. Nothing smaller than a cell conducts the basic functions associated with living. These functions include reproduction and the ability to take in nutrients. In the single minute that it took you to read these two paragraphs, the cells in your body probably conducted more than 1,000 biochemical reactions.

Born to Be Wild

One reason why cells are so active is that they are products of our ever-changing world. Scientists are not yet certain how the first cells formed, but one popular belief is the primordial soup theory. According to this theory, life began shortly after our planet formed more than 4.6 billion years ago. At that time, Earth's interior was full of hot molten

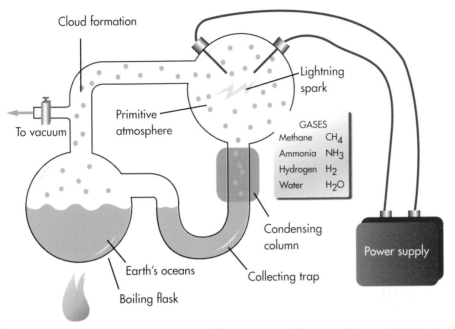

Cloud formation

Lightning
spark

Primitive
atmosphere

To vacuum

GASES
Methane CH_4
Ammonia NH_3
Hydrogen H_2
Water H_2O

Condensing
column

Power supply

Earth's oceans

Collecting trap

Boiling flask

An experiment conducted by Harold C. Urey and S. L. Miller in 1953 helped scientists illustrate how life originated on Earth. Simulating Earth's atmosphere before life existed by mixing heated water with methane, ammonia, and hydrogen gases—all plentiful in the atmosphere 4.6 billion years ago—and using an electric spark to mimic lightning, the scientists showed how amino acids were produced. Many proteins, carbohydrates, and nucleic acids essential to life are produced in the same way.

materials that shot explosively from the surface through numerous volcanoes and other surface openings. When the temperature dropped, scientists believe water vapors, or gases, in the atmosphere turned into showers heavier than any rains known today. These showers may have created the oceans. Water is key to the creation of life as we know it, so this torrential downpour likely set the stage for the birth of cells.

According to the primordial soup theory, the water became a liquid "broth" that could hold and react with simple organic molecules in Earth's early atmosphere. These molecules accumulated in the water, which increased their chances of meeting and combining. These natural combinations created the right conditions for life.

At around the same time, some science experts believe that tremendous bolts of lightning filled the skies. The force of the lightning may have discharged high voltage energy into Earth's atmospheric gases and water vapor. Cells may have spontaneously evolved in this highly charged environment, though it is very hard to know.

What Are Cells?

When cells first appeared on Earth, they were probably very simple structures made of linked

Fossilized evidence of a trilobite's exoskeleton (external skeleton) was found in a rock estimated to be more than 500 million years old. Trilobites, segmented arthropods that first appeared in the oceans about 540 million years ago during the Cambrian Period, were one of Earth's earliest life forms.

molecules that formed in and around semi-liquid droplets. Over time, molecules in the atmosphere and water may have served as catalysts. A catalyst is a substance that increases the rate of change of a chemical reaction without undergoing permanent change itself. Catalysts, along with continued activity and change in Earth's environment, may have allowed the simple first cells to evolve into higher, more complex forms of life. These structures then could have evolved into multicellular organisms, which led to life as we know it today.

The Cell Membrane

Cells can also be compared to the structure of the human body itself. Our bodies are covered with a protective skin that lets certain substances enter and exit. The cell membrane serves a similar purpose. It protects the contents of a cell and, like a gatekeeper, regulates what enters and exits the cell. Cell membranes are extremely small and thin. It would take about a million membranes stacked together to create a small speck, but their importance far exceeds their size. A cell could not exist without a membrane, just as humans and animals could not survive without skin.

Cell membranes are composed of a double layer of phospholipids, which are fatty substances not that different than fats and oils used for cooking foods. Under a microscope, a single phospholipid molecule looks a bit like a clothespin. Imagine two rows of

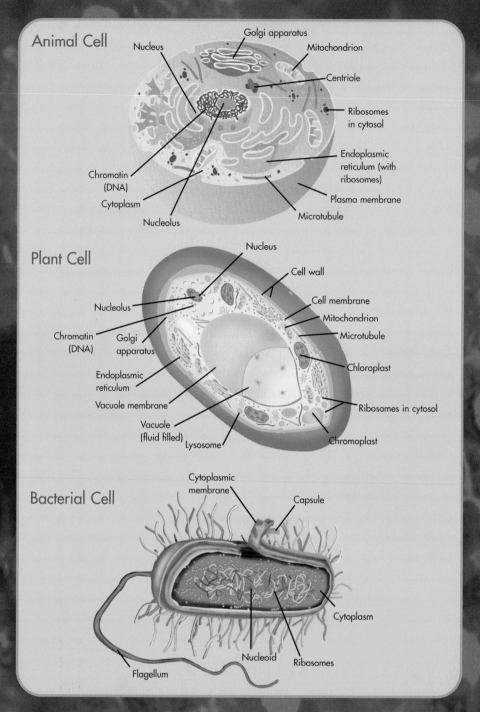

Animal Cell

Golgi apparatus

Nucleus

Mitochondrion

Centriole

Ribosomes
in cytosol

Endoplasmic
reticulum (with
ribosomes)

Chromatin
(DNA)

Cytoplasm

Plasma membrane

Nucleolus

Microtubule

Plant Cell

Nucleus

Cell wall

Cell membrane

Nucleolus

Mitochondrion

Microtubule

Chromatin
(DNA)

Golgi
apparatus

Chloroplast

Endoplasmic
reticulum

Ribosomes in cytosol

Vacuole membrane

Vacuole
(fluid filled)

Chromoplast

Lysosome

Bacterial Cell

Cytoplasmic
membrane

Capsule

Cytoplasm

Nucleoid

Ribosomes

Flagellum

The basic parts of eukaryotic and prokaryotic cells can be seen in these illustrations. Both animal and plant cells are eukaryotic because they have a nucleus, while bacterial cells are prokaryotic because they lack a true nucleus. While prokaryotes can be considered a more primitive life form, note the numerous organelles the plant and animal eukaryotes share.

clothespins lined up with the pointed ends all facing toward the middle. That is what the basic arrangement of a cell membrane looks like, except that the fatty molecules are suspended in a fluid structure. This suspension enables them to move around without losing their overall shape.

Similar to how your skin contains various pores and openings, the cell membrane has thousands of openings that control the flow of substances in and out of cells. These structures include receptors, channels, ports, and pumps. The latter three mostly allow for the easy movement of small, essential molecules, such as water and carbon dioxide, into cells.

When a cell does not have to expend energy to bring in a molecule, the process is called passive transport. Osmosis is an example of passive transport. Osmosis occurs when a liquid substance seeps into another area to maintain a balanced concentration of liquid in both areas. It allows a cell to equalize its liquid concentration, which mostly consists of water, with the liquid concentration found outside the cell. Cells use a similar process to keep oxygen and carbon dioxide amounts in check. Because of passive transport, it would be impossible for a cell to fill with oxygen and burst like a balloon, which does not have a permeable exterior.

Active transport requires energy. Cells use active transport to pull desired molecules inside the cell's interior. A salt molecule, for example, may approach the cell. If the cell needs sodium, a

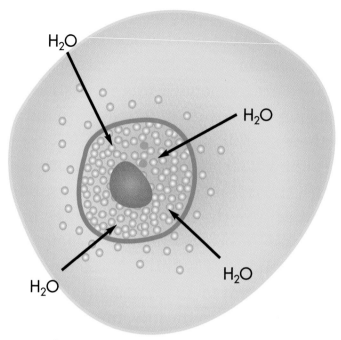

The process of osmosis, illustrated in this diagram, is the passage of water through a cell's semipermeable membrane. Osmosis is a form of passive transport. As water moves through the membrane, the cell swells. In human cells, excess water is secreted through the skin as sweat, or released by the body as liquid waste.

special receptor attaches itself to the salt molecule and pulls the molecule into the cell. There are receptors for many other types of molecules, including sugars and minerals. Any kind of action requires a fuel source, so the cell must expend a tiny bit of energy with each instance of active transport.

The Goal of Every Cell

The overall reason behind every cell function, including the transport of molecules, is to maintain a stable set of conditions within the cell. The water and oxygen levels, temperature, pressure, contents, and many

While some molecules, such as carbon dioxide and oxygen, can move through a cell's membrane without assistance, others rely upon a process known as active transport. In this illustration, molecules are transported by a carrier protein that is fueled by a source of outside energy. Only carrier proteins can support active transport.

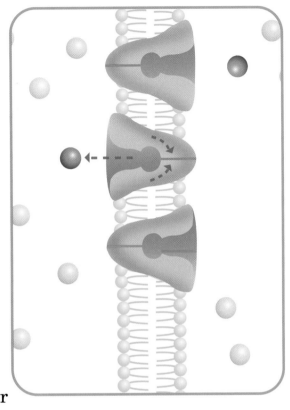

other factors must stay within a certain range, or else the cell could die. The same is true for a human being. If the imbalance becomes too great, a person could suffer illness or even death. Given all of the changes that occur within our bodies, it is no wonder that cells must constantly make adjustments and engage in other necessary activities in order to survive. The ability of a living organism to maintain stability is called homeostasis. The word homeostasis is derived from the Greek word *homoiosis*, which means "assimilation and resemblance." Homeostasis is the collective goal of all cells.

Chapter Two

Protein Builders

Similar to how your skin serves as an exterior boundary for your organs, the cell membrane serves as a boundary for organelles, or "little organs." Organelles are tiny structures within the cell that perform specific tasks, much in the same way that each of your organs has its own job in your body. The organelles and other parts of the cell are mostly made of protein.

You are probably familiar with the term protein in reference to one of the main food groups. Eggs, meat, fish, and dairy products are all high in protein. When studied at a smaller scale, the protein in these foods and in the organelles of your body's cells exist as organic compounds of molecules of amino acids. Broken down even further, amino acids consist of the elements carbon, hydrogen, nitrogen, oxygen, and sometimes sulfur. A single protein can usually be made from as few as two or as many as twenty different amino acids. Like the twenty-six-letter alphabet can make up different words and sentences, so can different amino acid combinations make up different proteins.

The word "unit" refers to distinct parts of the amino acids. In a protein, the amino acids become attached to each other through peptide bonds, which are like biochemical glue made from amino groups and carboxyl groups. Together, amino acid units form the protein that is in foods such as cheese and meat and the protein that makes up your cells.

More than 50 percent of the dry weight of our bodies, and that of other animals, is protein. There are many known proteins. Humans alone possess at least 30,000 to 40,000 different proteins. Out of this enormous number, most proteins fall into two distinct groups: fibrous and globular.

Fibrous Proteins

Distinct conditions determine whether a protein is fibrous or globular. These factors include how the amino acids are bonded together, and how the bonds are shaped and electrically charged (either by positive or negative atom forces). Fibrous proteins tend to be stable structures that don't react much with other molecules. Collagen, for example, is a fibrous protein. It makes up your bone, cartilage, skin, and tendons. Collagen contains more than 1,000 amino acids linked together to form long strands. This arrangement and composition gives collagen its strength and flexibility. Gelatin is made from collagen fibrils that have been broken down by boiling.

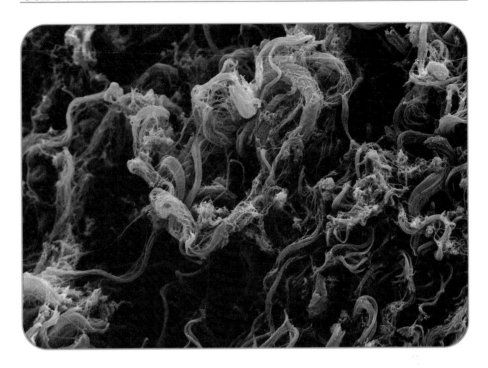

Collagen, seen in this scanning electron micrograph, is the most abundant protein in the body, comprising about one-fourth of all its protein. Collagen forms the major parts of human bones, tendons, and body tissues and helps form the connective tissue between bones. As a protein that is supported by vitamin C, those people with vitamin C deficiencies risk a breakdown in collagen that usually results in scurvy.

Muscle proteins, fibrogen, and keratin are three other types of fibrous proteins. Keratin is the protein in your hair and nails. It also makes up the feathers, hooves, and scales of birds, horses, fish, and other animals. Keratin is a very stable protein that does not dissolve in water. This is a good thing when you consider how many times a week you wash your hair and hands! Permanents that cause hair to curl use chemicals to break the bonds in keratin, causing the protein fibers to soften and become more twisted in shape.

Globular Proteins

While fibrous proteins tend to be strong and stable, globular proteins dissolve easily in liquids. Globular proteins react more with other substances surrounding them. Both blood and milk contain globular proteins. Eggs also contain albumin, a kind of globular protein. In milk and eggs, water-soluble proteins are suspended in a liquid mixture. In blood, the globular protein called hemoglobin holds oxygen and gives blood its distinctive red color.

Globular proteins fall into five main groups: antibodies, microtubules, protein hormones, enzymes, and actin filaments. All of these proteins have functions that require interaction with their surroundings. Enzymes are especially important to cell functions because they serve as catalysts for many cellular chemical reactions. Most enzymes can do this because they contain slots that fit other molecules. A substance may float by and a molecule from it could slip into a slot especially designed to target this particular molecule on the enzyme. Another slot could attract some other molecule. Before long, the molecules may join to trigger a chemical reaction.

We take in both fibrous and globular protein in our food, but we also assemble our own proteins. This manufacturing process is called protein synthesis. It is one of the most important functions carried out in all cells. The boss of the whole job is deoxyribonucleic acid, or DNA.

Deoxyribonucleic Acid (DNA)

DNA, the chemical that makes up chromosomes, contains the master plan for everything about a person or any other living thing. A person is made from nearly the same basic cellular components as a plant is, but DNA in humans ensures that the first two cells that multiply into the trillions create the correct proteins.

Human DNA contains the blueprint for human beings. While scientists do not yet fully understand everything about the genetic code, which is the plan embedded within DNA, it is believed that information going back to prehistoric times is imprinted in the code, but has been rendered unusable by humans today. For example, DNA may still contain instructions to make humans fully covered with hair. Over long periods, these instructions evolved to create who we are today.

Because DNA is so important, it is locked away in a special part of the cell called the cell nucleus. The nucleus has its own membrane. Like the main cell membrane, the nuclear membrane serves as a protective barrier. It allows certain select visitors to come in and out. The molecules of DNA lie on chromosomes, which are thin structures that look like two intertwined ladders. Amazingly, each cell contains approximately six feet (1.8 meters) of DNA packed into the nucleus.

The sides of the DNA ladder are made out of sugars and phosphates. They hold the rungs of the

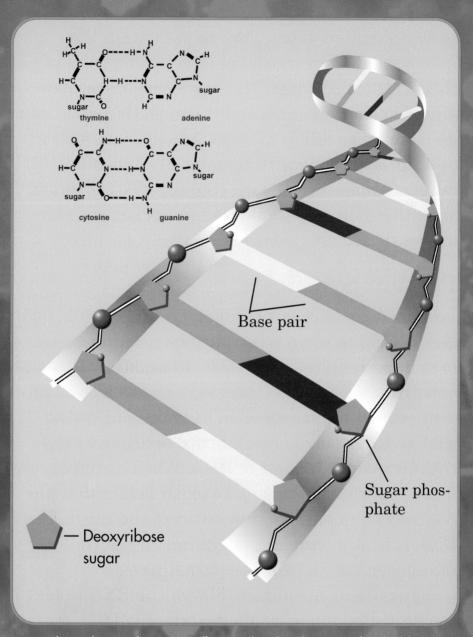

Base pair

Sugar phos-
phate

Deoxyribose
sugar

Deoxyribonucleic acid (DNA) is illustrated in this diagram of a double helix structure. DNA is responsible for storing the genetic information that is carried from an individual's parents, the same information that determines human traits such as eye and hair color, how tall you will become, and your potential to develop certain inherited diseases. This information is contained in four nitrogen bases: thymine, adenine, cytosine, and guanine. Together, these bases match to form base pairs *(upper left)*. These base pairs are held together by a sugar phosphate backbone, creating the double helix structure.

ladder shape in place. The rungs contain the information. They consist of interlocking pairs of chemicals called bases. There are four bases: adenine, cytosine, guanine, and thymine. Bases can pair up in only two different ways. Adenine, abbreviated as A, always bonds with thymine (T). Cytosine (C), in turn, always bonds with guanine (G). The amino acids that make up protein consist of various pairings of these four chemicals.

Protein Synthesis

Proteins help to repair organelles in cells, build body tissues, and to serve other purposes. Because protein is so important, cells assemble it out of raw ingredients. This construction process is known as protein synthesis. It begins when an enzyme (ribonucleic acid, or RNA, polymerase) unzips apart and copies the intertwined ladders of DNA. When unzipped, an individual chromosome looks like a ladder that has been sawed in half lengthwise down the rungs. The DNA acts as a template to synthesize a portable messenger known as messenger RNA (mRNA).

The nuclear membrane allows the RNA to leave the protected nucleus. Meanwhile, the DNA zips back together again to secure its valuable codes. The mRNA travels to molecular machines known as ribosomes. If DNA is the boss for protein synthesis, then ribosomes are the factory and its workers. Ribosomes are located on a network of membranes that folds through the jellylike liquid,

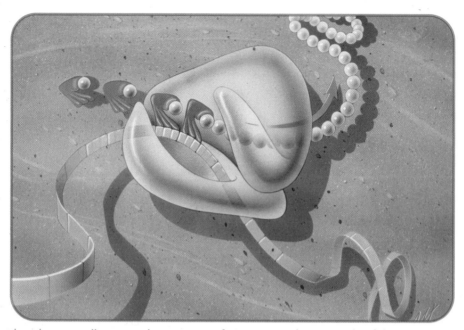

This diagram illustrates the process of protein synthesis. Each of the twenty amino acids from which protein is built must be attached to its specific transfer RNA (tRNA) molecule and the subunits of the ribosome (colored blue) on which the new protein is to be made. Protein synthesis occurs when all of these components come together in the cell's cytoplasm to form a functional ribosome. In this image, amino acids carried by tRNA are colored red while the polypeptide chain is colored pink.

the cytoplasm that fills much of a cell's interior. This network of membranes is called the endoplasmic reticulum. Some parts of it are smooth, while others look rough under a microscope. The roughness comes from numerous ribosomes dotted along the folds.

The ribosome recognizes mRNA and moves it along to read and decode its information. The ribosome triggers another kind of RNA, transfer RNA, to collect the bases of amino acids, located in the cytoplasm. These amino acids are necessary to make up the protein encoded on the messenger.

Imagine a children's toy in which blocks of different shapes can fit into only certain shaped holes or grooves. A triangle block, for example, can only fit into a triangular hole. That is similar to how transfer RNA lines up molecules on the mold formed by the messenger RNA. Each coding segment on the mold is divided into three slots for chemical bases. A single segment is called a codon. It takes three bases, or nucleotides, to make up one amino acid. When a transfer RNA does its job, it is set free to search for more amino acid parts. The amino acids line up on the messenger RNA and form peptide bonds as each amino acid is brought in. The process is repeated many times, as proteins consist of numerous groupings of amino acids.

At the end of the cycle, the final codon signals to the ribosome that the protein is finished. Some proteins remain in the cell because they are needed for organelle replacement and repair while others wait for further processing before export.

Chapter Three

Cell Processes and Movement

At any given moment, the cells in your body are building proteins and processing them for use in and out of the cell. Proteins are not the only things in motion. Cells themselves can move around, just as you can move your arms, legs, and other parts of your body. At this very minute, some of your body's cells may be zipping through your lungs, blood, and other sites to chase down and destroy unwanted invaders. For example, you may have unknowingly breathed in a particle of dust. Cells can destroy foreign substances, such as dust or bacteria. If the dust makes its way to your lungs, warriorlike cells could find and destroy it.

Proteins in Motion

When a ribosome completes a cycle of protein synthesis, proteins leave the ribosomes on the endoplasmic reticulum and enter the part of the cell known as the Golgi apparatus. This is an organelle made up of several stacked chambers that resemble deflated balloons when viewed

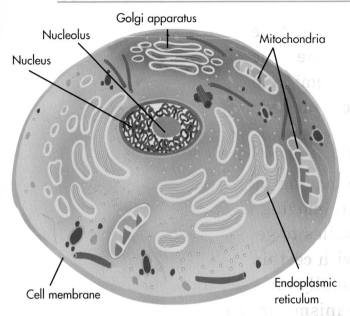

Nucleolus

Golgi apparatus

Nucleus

Mitochondria

Cell membrane

Endoplasmic reticulum

The center of the eukaryotic cell contains the nucleus, the control center, and the nucleolus, which houses genetic material. The cell's mitochondria help it generate energy. The endoplasmic reticulum performs the job of synthesizing proteins and sending them to the Golgi apparatus, the organelle responsible for routing them to other areas within the cell.

under a microscope. The Golgi apparatus contains enzymes that add finishing touches to proteins. Sometimes proteins will gain atoms, such as phosphorus or sulfur, to tailor them for use in the body. Other times, small bits of the protein made by the ribosome will be chopped off.

When a protein travels through one compartment of the Golgi apparatus, the protein is encased in a vesicle. Vesicles are tiny, membrane-enclosed containers. They are the cells' "shipping boxes." The protein moves from chamber to chamber within the organelle until it is ready to be "shipped" to various parts of the body.

During the protein-making process in the ribosome, certain amino acids within the protein serve as "shipping labels." These amino acids may exist in groups of four to 100, depending on where the protein should go. Proteins destined for use in the cell simply leave the Golgi and take their place within the cell. Others carrying their molecular label leave the cell through its membrane. They journey until they reach their programmed location.

Cell Movement

While proteins are moving in and out of cells, certain cells also are moving in place, or are traveling around our bodies to get nutrients, target enemies, or meet with certain cells. Cells within the human body usually move by three mechanisms. These mechanisms are cilia, flagella, and amoeboid motion.

Cilia are small, hairlike wisps made by basal bodies. Basal bodies are tiny structures located on the insides of cell membranes. These structures make cilia out of protein. The protein hairs shoot out through the cell membranes of many cells. Under a microscope, these cells look furry because of the presence of numerous cilia. Cilia work like old-fashioned ships powered by an oar-wielding crew. With every stroke, the cilia beat in time to either glide themselves, or to move surrounding particles away from the cell.

Flagella are single, long structures resembling tails. Like cilia, flagella also are made out of protein. Cells with a flagellum whip it up and down. Like a fish that glides through water by moving its tail, the cell can then glide over relatively long distances using a flagellum.

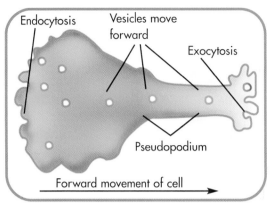

A pseudopodium *(left)*, or "false foot," is one mechanism cells use in amoeboid motion. The unicellular amoeba is able to move because its cytoplasm projects outward (exocytosis) and is followed by the rest of the cell. Endocytosis is the process when the rest of the cell joins with the pseudopodium, enabling it to move forward. On the right is an illustration of cilia, the microscopic hairlike wisps that project from the cell membrane of some eukaryotic cells, another mechanism that cells use to travel.

Amoeboid motion is a technical term for crawling. Instead of using arms and legs, however, cells such as white blood cells, use pseudopodia, which means "false feet." The pseudopodia are extended portions of the cytoplasm that remain enclosed by the cell's membrane. Think of pseudopodia like toes that stick out of feet. The false feet move in a slow crawling motion that is an effective and strong form of traveling.

Seek and Destroy

Crawling white blood cells combat invaders. As we interact with our environment, our bodies can become exposed to dangerous invaders. These unwanted guests can range from a seemingly harmless grain of pollen to bacteria to killer viruses. We may breathe these substances in the air, or ingest parasitic organisms into our bodies by eating or drinking contaminated food or water.

Cells, such as white blood cells, and macrophages, which are free-roaming cells that eat unwanted foreign substances such as dust or bacteria, come to our rescue. The word "macrophage" means "big eater." One job of macrophages is to clean up old red blood cells out of our bloodstream. In a typical day, macrophages consume 100 billion of your old red blood cells.

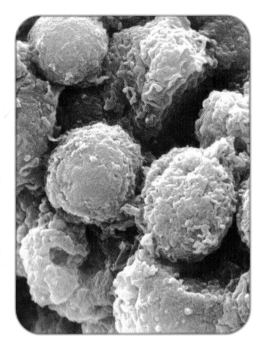

This colored scanning electron micrograph shows a group of white blood cells, or leukocytes. White blood cells defend the body against infection by ingesting foreign materials (antigens) and destroying harmful growth, such as the development and spread of cancer cells. Human blood comprises white and red blood cells (erythrocytes), platelets, and plasma.

Lysosomes

Macrophages and other cells are able to eat and destroy invaders chiefly because of an organelle called a lysosome. Lysosomes are vesicles full of enzymes that exist in a cell's cytoplasm. They serve as the "stomach" of the cell.

To kill an outside invader, a search and destroy cell is able to open up its membrane around the

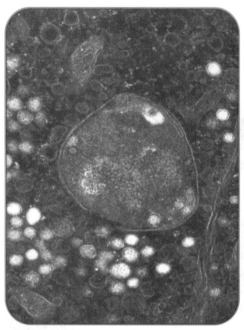

Lysosomes, like the darkened body in this microscopic image, are the cell's organelles responsible for digesting organic material, such as old cell parts. Filled with enzymes, each membrane-bound lysosome is like a tiny stomach within the cell's cytoplasm that helps it rid itself of waste.

unwanted guest, such as a bacterium, and enclose the intruder within the cell. Once there, lysosomes that are manufactured by the Golgi apparatus and the endoplasmic reticulum break down the invader into components. These remaining bits, like garbage, can be recycled for later use by the cell.

Lysosomes also digest old organelles, cell pollution, such as leftover oxygen molecules, and other unnecessary and potentially dangerous substances within a cell. Sometimes lysosomes are assisted by peroxisomes, which help break down alcohol, certain bacteria, oxygen, and even harmful drugs. When a person consumes a lot of alcohol or harmful drugs, he or she puts an enormous burden on organelles such as lysosomes and peroxisomes. Sometimes this burden becomes too much, and damage or death not only of the individual cells, but of the human consumer, may occur.

Chapter Four

Mini Power Stations

Seek and destroy missions, protein synthesis, and other cellular activities require a lot of energy. Just as a car needs fuel in order to run, cells need fuel to conduct most of their functions. According to the laws of science, living organisms cannot create or destroy energy, but they can transform it from one kind of energy into another kind. That is what cells and all other living organisms do. The primary energy source for everything alive on Earth is the Sun.

Photosynthesis

The life of a leafy vegetable might seem to be separate from that of a human cell, but the story of how human cells become energized begins with plants. All green plants can convert the energy from light into food. In nature, this light shines down from the Sun, but the light can also come from artificial sources, such as a sun lamp. Green plants convert light energy into a chemical form that can be stored for later use. The chemical form is food, and the process of conversion is photosynthesis. Photosynthesis is derived from the Greek word "phos," meaning light, and "syn," meaning together.

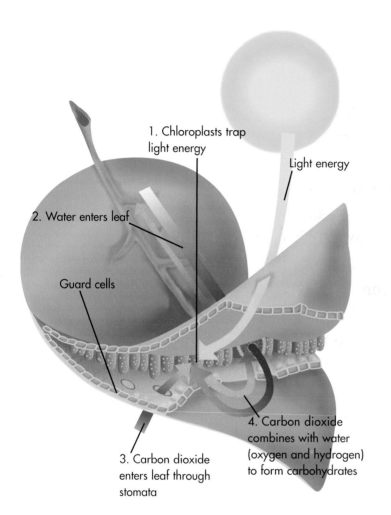

1. Chloroplasts trap light energy

Light energy

2. Water enters leaf

Guard cells

3. Carbon dioxide enters leaf through stomata

4. Carbon dioxide combines with water (oxygen and hydrogen) to form carbohydrates

This diagram illustrates how chlorophyll-containing cells within green leaves absorb sunlight. Plants transform sunlight into chemical energy during photosynthesis. The photosynthesis process captures sunlight and uses it to transform water and carbon dioxide into sugar and oxygen, which is then given off as a waste product.

During photosynthesis, a green pigment in plants called chlorophyll absorbs light. Organelles within the chlorophyll, called chloroplasts, split molecules of water within the plant into their basic components of hydrogen and oxygen. Most of the oxygen on Earth is derived from plants. That is one reason why other planets in our solar system seem to lack large quantities of oxygen. They have no apparent plants to release it.

Houseplant Benefits

Plants have a unique ability to give off oxygen and absorb certain harmful substances in the air. Both of these qualities allow many indoor plants to serve as natural air purifiers, in addition to what they add in terms of beauty.

There may also be some benefit to talking to your plants. When we speak, we give off carbon dioxide and moisture from our breath. Plants use both water and carbon dioxide to make food.

The hydrogen from the split molecules of water, which is absorbed from the plant's soil, combines with carbon dioxide to form a simple sugar called glucose. With a few extra ingredients, such as nitrogen, phosphorus, and sulfur, glucose can then be transformed by the plant into other forms of food, such as protein, amino acids, fat, and vitamins.

Glucose

Glucose provides the main source of food energy for most living organisms on Earth. Foods such as honey and grapes are loaded with glucose, but you can obtain glucose through the consumption of meat. That is because at some point, the animal that provided the meat ate plant material, or down the food chain, some other organism that it ate consumed a basic sugar.

Even foods that do not seem sweet can be high in glucose. Potatoes, for example, are rich in carbohydrates, which the human body breaks down into glucose and other molecules. The potato plant uses this tuber as a big storehouse for food derived from light energy.

ATP

While tasty and sweet, the sugar glucose by itself could not be used by our bodies as fuel. We must first convert it into a compound known as ATP, which stands for adenosine triphosphate. The chemical name refers to the fact that ATP consists of a molecule of adenosine that has bonded with three molecules of phosphate. The prefix "tri" means "three."

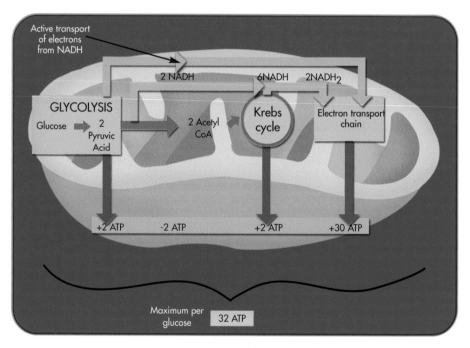

Although the process of converting glucose begins with glycolysis (combining it with enzymes and acids), the ATP (adenosine triphosphate) created by the chemical reaction is maximized in the second step of the process called the Krebs cycle. This efficient production of ATP during the Krebs cycle takes place within the cell's mitochondria.

ATP works like a battery for most activities conducted in a cell. The energy of ATP is stored in the chemical bonds that link the phosphate molecules to the adenosine. All chemical bonds occur because of forces that hold atoms together. Just as the batteries that we use to run our radios and high-tech gadgets have a negative and a positive charge, atoms possess these charges, too. Strong electrical charges bond each phosphate within ATP. When one or more of the bonds is broken, the stored electricity is released as energy.

The Cell's Power Plants

Mitochondria serve as a cell's power plants. They transform glucose into energy-rich ATP. Mitochondria are organelles found in the cytoplasm of cells. The outside of a mitochondrion organelle consists of a smooth outer membrane made of protein molecules. Inside is another membrane with flowing folds called cristae. Cristae are the places where ATP is synthesized. They are folded because that increases the work surface area, which allows for more space to make ATP.

Mitochondria could represent some of the oldest surviving things on Earth. Unlike other cell organelles, mitochondria have their own stores of DNA and ribosomes. They are almost like mini cells within cells. Their unique structure has led many scientists to believe that mitochondria evolved millions of years ago and were then engulfed by larger cells.

The two cells then may have developed a working relationship whereby the mitochondria provided energy while the larger host cell provided nutrients and protection. The cell that was swallowed up could have evolved into what we now know as mitochondria.

Some parts of the body have more mitochondria than others. That is because these parts require greater energy sources. Muscles, like those in your heart, have large numbers of mitochondria within their cells. The liver needs plenty of these organelles because the liver requires a lot of energy to detoxify and regulate blood, hormones, excess sugars, and other substances in our bodies.

How Mitochondria Make Energy

The energy-making process that takes place mostly in the mitochondria is called cell respiration. During cell respiration, chemical reactions within a cell transform glucose into ATP. It takes three chemical reactions to get the most energy out of a glucose molecule. In order, these reactions are glycolysis, the Krebs cycle, and the electron transportation system.

A cell first starts out with molecules of glucose. The glucose, from food sources, enters the cell through the cell membrane and winds up in the jellylike cytoplasm. The glucose that enters the cell consists of six carbons. In the cytoplasm, each glucose molecule is split in half, leaving two three-carbon fragments. The breaking of the carbon bonds produces some ATP, but not very much, so the process continues. The next step in the transformation of glucose is called the Krebs cycle.

The Krebs cycle was named after its discoverer, Hans Krebs, a German-born British biochemist. Krebs observed that the three-carbon fragments produced a substance called pyruvic acid that could be transported to the mitochondria. In the mitochondria, the pyruvic acid reacts with water. A chemical reaction causes the mixture of water and pyruvic acid to produce carbon dioxide and ten hydrogen atoms. The hydrogen atoms then move away to the cristae, where they enter the cristae's electron transport chain.

Depending on the type of cell, its mitochondria are located in strategic places to maximize the production of energy for that cell. In this example of a cardiac muscle cell *(top)*, mitochondria are located close to where the muscle contracts. The ATP produced in the mitochondria supports the constant involuntary contraction of the heart muscle. In the sperm cell *(bottom)*, the mitochondria are located in the flagellum, the "tail" responsible for the sperm's movement.

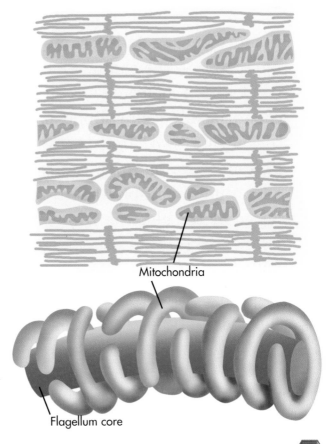

Mitochondria

Flagellum core

Hydrogen atoms contain a positively charged particle called a proton and a negatively charged particle called an electron. The electron transport chain separates these electrons and protons from each hydrogen atom. The protons are eventually made into water, which is a by-product of the process. Our bodies also release heat as a by-product of all of these biochemical reactions. That is one reason why humans stay warm and release moisture through such acts as breathing and perspiring.

The electrons separated from the hydrogen continue their journey down the electron transport chain. As they move along the various knobs and folds of the cristae, they react with oxygen atoms to produce energy. At the same time, protons are pumped into the chain, which causes phosphate to bond with a molecule already present in the mitochondria, adenosine diphosphate (ADP). The prefix "di" means "two." In this case, the prefix signifies that only two phosphates are bonded to adenosine in adenosine diphosphate. The electron energy produced by the electron transport cycle allows another phosphate to bond with the adenosine. This makes ATP. The three-part energy process turns a single molecule of glucose into more than thirty ATP molecules of energy.

Metabolism

When a cell makes energy, it must break complex units into simpler units, such as the glucose being transformed into pyruvic acid. This breaking down of materials is known as destructive metabolism, or catabolism. Conversely, when a cell turns a smaller unit into a larger, more complex one, this is called constructive metabolism, or anabolism. Ribosomes, for example, construct protein out of amino acids. Together, the processes of anabolism and catabolism make up metabolism.

You probably are familiar with the term "metabolism" in reference to a person's weight. People who tend to eat a lot but do not put on pounds are often said to have a high metabolic rate. Other people may not eat much, but still gain weight. They could have a lower metabolic rate. Just as the goal of all cells is to achieve homeostasis, one of the primary goals of our bodies is to achieve a balance between anabolism and catabolism. Once this goal has been achieved, a person is said to be in a state of dynamic equilibrium, which means that he or she has a healthy and balanced metabolism.

Chapter Five

Specialized Cells

Protein building and energy production occur in every human cell, but some functions are restricted to certain types of cells. There are approximately 200 types of specialized cells within our bodies. Five general groups of specialized cells are nerve cells, eye cells, ear cells, nose cells, and secretory cells. All have membranes that enclose both their nucleus and their cytoplasm filled with organelles, but they may have additional features or extra organelles to accomplish their necessary work.

Nerve Cells

In addition to possessing the basic cell body, nerve cells have numerous dendrites and an axon. Dendrites are hairlike projections that act like mini receiver antennae. Chemical signals, sent by other nerve cells, are picked up by dendrites. For example, if you touch the tip of your finger to this book now, many dendrites in nerve cells within your fingertip will send messages to help process the information about how the book feels.

An axon serves as the cell's transmitter. Axons are full of special micro-tubules that allow electrical signals to pass on to dendrites. An act as simple as touching your finger to this book requires communication between many nerve cell axons and dendrites. Eye and ear cells are also con-sidered nerve cells.

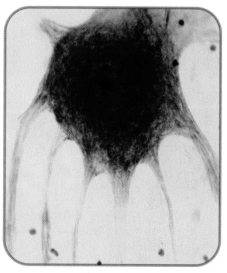

Components of a neuron, or nerve cell, are visible in this microscopic image. Each neuron contains a cell body; an axon, the electrical "conduc-tor" that sends information between neurons; the branchlike dendrites, the receivers of that information; and a nucleus, the cell's control center. Each human brain houses about a hundred billion neurons.

Eye Cells

The human eye, which translates light into multidimensional images perceived in the brain, contains many different kinds of specialized cells. Two are rod and cone cells. As their names suggest, rod cells are relatively long and narrow, while cone cells look a bit like a cone-shaped hair comb when magnified.

Rod cells are incredibly sensitive. They can detect a single photon of light. However, it takes at least five or more photons before we register having seen anything. A rod cell's cellular tool kit includes a photoreceptor pigment that allows for light detection and an axon, which is a support center within the cell.

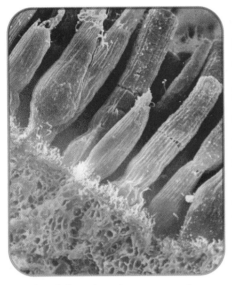

This brightly colored scanning electron micrograph shows the rods (blue) and cones (green-blue) within the retina of a human eye. Both rod and cone cells are highly specialized light-sensitive cells located on the surface of the retina. Together, rod and cone cells detect visual images, which are then transmitted as nerve impulses to the optic nerve and the brain.

Cone cells also have an axon but, unlike rod cells, they have a larger nucleus, more mitochondria, and a different-shaped photo-receptor pigment region. These differences enable photoreceptive molecules within the cone cells to detect colors, while rod cells work only in black and white. Rod cells are more sensitive to light than cone cells, which is why it is hard to see colors under low light conditions.

Ear Cells

Cells designed for hearing also possess a particular kind of cilia called stereocilia. Unlike most other cilia in the body, stereocilia are equipped with protein fibers instead of microtubules. The fibrous construction enables stereocilia to stimulate the nerve cells to which they are attached. The stimulus takes the form of a nerve impulse that eventually travels to the brain. Similar to how the brain interprets odors, it also must translate these nerve impulses from the ear into sound.

Human ear cells have evolved over thousands of years, during which time there were no rock concerts, televisions, or headphones. As a result, our ears are designed to hear sound at reasonable levels. After a loud concert, perhaps you have experienced ear ringing. If so, that means that some of your stereocilia were damaged. Over time, such damage can cause hearing loss. That is why many performers wear earplugs to help protect their ability to hear.

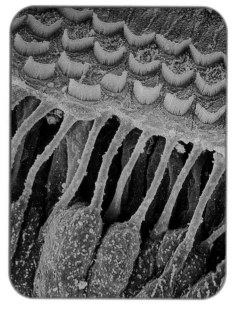

Hair cells of a healthy human ear are colored brown and pink in this scanning electron micrograph. The inner ear converts sound waves into nerve impulses by stimulation of stereocilia (pink) projections at the ends of the hair cells.

Nose Cells

Nose cells contain modified cilia that sway back and forth in response to stimulation by odor molecules. When you smell a flower, for example, cilia in cells within your nose capture odor molecules from that flower and position them toward the roof of the nose to your skull and brain. The brain then processes these molecules into a fragrance or odor.

Cilia are also useful for whisking air pollutants, such as molecules of mold, dust, and dirt, out of your nose. The unwanted molecules will be coated with nasal mucus, which allows them to slide down your throat for eventual disposal from your body.

Secretory Cells

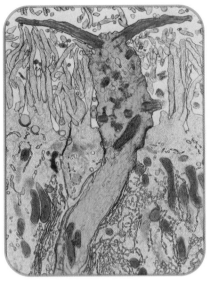

This colored transmission electron micrograph shows a section of the olfactory (smell) epithelium of the human nose. The center (orange) section is an olfactory cell body. Two long nonmoving cilia hairs project into the liquid lining of the nasal cavity.

The word "secretory" comes from the word "secrete," which means "to send out." Secretory cells, therefore, are responsible for secreting substances both inside and outside of your body. Certain cells within your eyes, for example, excrete tears to lubricate the eye. The liquid lubricant contains water, along with components that help protect the eye against infection. Secretory cells possess very active Golgi bodies. These organelles stay busy by secreting digestive enzymes into the stomach, hormones into our bloodstream, the salty fluid known as sweat out of our pores, and other substances.

The Dynamic Cell

Cells pack a great deal of action and power into a very small space. Red blood cells only measure 0.00003 inches in length, yet they can move, generate their own power, synthesize proteins, digest and recycle cell garbage, and conduct many more activities. Cells can even make copies of themselves through mitosis, a process of cell reproduction. You and all other human

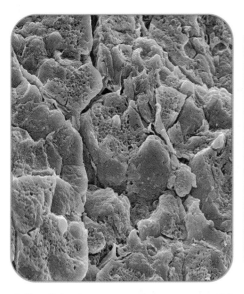 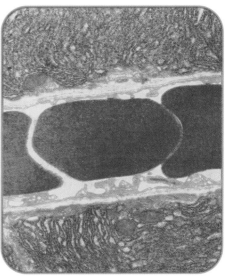

Cells of the human pancreas are visible in this colored scanning electron micrograph *(left)*. These cells secrete an enzyme-rich fluid into the small intestine through the pancreatic duct. Once there, they help the body process proteins, lipids (fats), and carbohydrates. The red blood cells *(right)* in this transmission electron micrograph are inside a capillary. Red blood cells, also called erythrocytes, distribute oxygen throughout the body.

beings began from single cells that replicated many times to create the body you have today.

Cells are dynamic structures that were born out of change and constant activity. Their seemingly tireless level of energy mirrors that of our spinning planet. Because nature is in a continual state of change, so, too, are cells. Perhaps a cell's most impressive function is its ability to evolve over time. Life as we know it began as simple, single-celled creatures that evolved into complex forms, such as humans and other animals. If nothing disrupts this evolutionary process, cells will continue to function, thrive, and perfect themselves for the future benefit of all living organisms.

Glossary

active transport (AK-tiv tranz-PORT) The cell's use of energy to bring in a molecule.

ATP (adenosine triphosphate) (ah-den-oo-ZEEN try-FOS-fayt) A compound that contains stored energy and is the main source of fuel for cells.

axon (AX-on) The transmitter portion of a nerve cell.

bases (BAY-siz) Interlocking chemicals in DNA that contain vital information about a cell.

carboxyl (kar-BOX-uhl) An organic acid involved in the construction of proteins.

catalyst (kat-uh-LIST) A substance that increases the rate of change of a reaction without undergoing permanent change itself.

cell membrane (SEL MEM-brayn) A thin, semipermeable double layer of fatty molecules that surrounds every cell body.

chromosome (KROH-muh-sohm) A strand made of DNA that contains a portion of the hereditary information of a cell; humans have forty-six chromosomes.

cilia (SIH-lee-uh) Small hairlike objects that extend outward through the membrane of some cells to help them move.

codon (ko-DON) A group of three nucleotides that codes for one amino acid.

cone cell (KOHN SEL) A specialized eye cell that allows humans and other non-colorblind animals to see in color.

cristae (KRIH-stay) Inner folds within a mitochondria where ATP synthesis takes place.

cytoplasm (SY-toh-plah-zum) The gelatinous liquid substance within a cell's interior.

dendrite (den-DRIGHT) A hairlike projection from nerve cells that receives information.

DNA (deoxyribonucleic acid) (dee-ahk-see-ry-BOH-noo-klay-ik AH-sid) The chemical that makes up chromosomes.

electron (ih-LEK-tron) The negatively charged particle of an atom.

endoplasmic reticulum (EN-doh-plahs-mik reh-TIH-kyoo-lum) A network of membranes within a cell; it houses ribosomes, which are involved in the building of proteins.

fibrous proteins (FY-ber-us PROH-teenz) Proteins that have a stable structure and tend not to react with other molecules, such as collagen, keratin, and muscle proteins.

flagella (fluh-JEL-uh) Tail-like objects that enable some cells, such as sperm, to travel.

globular proteins (glob-U-lur PROH-teenz) Proteins that can dissolve in liquids and react easily with other molecules, such as hemoglobin in blood, that react with oxygen in the lungs and carry it around the body.

glucose (GLOO-kohs) A simple sugar that is the product of photosynthesis.

Golgi apparatus (GOHL-jee ah-pahr-AH-tus) An organelle that handles protein processing and transport.

homeostasis (hohm-ee-oh-STAY-sis) A state of stability that a living cell or organism works to maintain; it is the collective goal of all cells.

lysosome (LY-so-zohm) Vesicle full of enzymes that enables a cell to break down certain molecules for recycling or disposal.

macrophages (mah-CROW-fah-jiz) Free-roaming cells that eat up unwanted molecules such as bacteria.

messenger RNA (meh-SIN-jer RNA) A chemical that represents a mobile copy of a region of DNA that can move out of the nucleus and code for a protein made in the cytoplasm. (RNA is an acronym for ribonucleic acid.)

metabolism (meh-TA-buh-lih-zum) A process of catabolism, the breaking down of substances into smaller units, and anabolism, the construction of substances from smaller units.

mitochondrion (MY-toh-kon-dree-un) The organelle that is primarily responsible for ATP synthesis.

nucleotide (NOO-klee-oh-tyd) One unit within a strand of DNA.

nucleus (NOO-klee-us) An interior portion of a cell that consists mainly of chromosomes and is protected by its own membrane.

passive transport (pah-SIV tranz-PORT) A cell's gathering of a molecule without having to expend energy.

peptide bonds (PEP-tyd BONDZ) Links made of amino and carboxyl within a protein that hold amino acids together like glue.

phospholipids (fos-foh-lip-IDZ) Fatty substances that make up cell membranes.

photosynthesis (foh-toh-SIN-thuh-sis) The process by which green plants convert the energy of sunlight into food.

protein (PROH-teen) A complex organic compound that contains amino acids as their basic structural units.

protein synthesis (PROH-teen SIN-thuh-sis) The process by which cells construct proteins out of amino acids using messenger RNA as the instruction manual.

proton (PROH-ton) The positive charge of an atom.

ribosome (RY-boh-zohm) Cell organelle that is responsible for protein synthesis.

RNA (ribonucleic acid) (RY-boh-noo-klay-ik AH-sid) A molecule involved in protein synthesis.

rod cells (ROD SELZ) Eye cells that detect low levels of light and transmit information in black and white.

secretory cells (SEE-kree-tor-ee SELZ) Cells that are responsible for secreted substances both inside and outside of your body.

transfer RNA (TRANZ-fur RNA) A chemical that gathers amino acids for use in creating proteins.

For More Information

Cell Magazine
1100 Massachusetts Avenue
Cambridge, MA 02138
(617) 661-7057
Web site: http://www.cell.com

Discover Magazine
114 Fifth Avenue
New York, NY 10011
(212) 633-4400
Web site: http://www.discover.com

eBioiMEDIA
P.O. Box 1234
Beaufort, SC 29901-1234
(877) 661-5355
Web site: http://ebiomedia.com

Web Sites

Due to the changing nature of Internet links, the Rosen Publishing Group, Inc., has developed an online list of Web sites related to the subject of this book. This site is updated regularly. Please use this link to access the list:

http://www.rosenlinks.com/lce/cefu

For Further Reading

Balkwill, Francis R. *Enjoy Your Cells.* Cold Spring Harbor,
NY: Cold Spring Harbor Laboratory Press, 2002.

Claybourne, Anna. *The Complete Book of the Human
Body*. New York: Usborne Publishing, Inc., 2004.

Gareth Stevens Publishing. *Genetics.* Milwaukee, WI:
Gareth Stevens Publishing, 2003.

Walker, Richard. *Genes and DNA* (Kingfisher Knowledge
Series). New York: Houghton Mifflin Company, 2003.

Bibliography

Clark, John. *The Cell: A Small Wonder.* New York: Torstar
Books, Inc., 1985.

Fichter, George S. *Cells.* New York: Franklin Watts, 1986.

National Geographic Society. *The Incredible Machine.*
Washington, D.C.: National Geographic Society, 1994.

Parker, Steve. *How the Body Works.* New York: Reader's
Digest Association, 1994.

Rensberger, Boyce. *Life Itself: Exploring the Realm of the
Living Cell.* New York: Oxford University Press, 1996.

Roca, Nuria. *Cells, Genes, and Chromosomes.* New York:
Chelsea House Publishers, 1996.

Walker, Richard. *Encyclopedia of the Human Body.* New
York: DK Publishing, Inc., 2002.

Whitfield, Philip. *The Human Body Explained: A Guide to
Understanding the Incredible Living Machine.* New
York: Henry Holt and Company, 1995.

Young, John K. *Cells: Amazing Forms and Functions.*
New York: Franklin Watts, 1990.

Index

A
active transport, 9–10
adenosine diphosphate (ADP), 34
adenosine triphosphate (ATP), 30–31, 32, 34
amino acids, 12–13, 18, 20, 22, 29, 35

C
cell membrane, 7–10, 12, 16, 23, 32
cell movement, 23–24
cell respiration, 32
chromosomes, 16, 18

D
DNA (deoxyribonucleic acid), 15, 16–18, 31

E
ear cells, 38–39
electron transportation system, 32, 34
endoplasmic reticulum, 19, 21, 26
eye cells, 37–38

G
glucose, 29–30, 32, 33, 34–35
glycolysis, 32
Golgi apparatus, 21–23, 26, 40

H
homeostasis, 11, 35

K
Krebs cycle, 32, 33

L
lysosomes, 25–26

M
macrophages, 25
messenger RNA (mRNA), 18, 19, 20
metabolism, 34–35
mitochondria, 31–32, 33, 34

N
nerve cells, 36–37
nose cells, 39
nuclear membrane, 16, 18
nucleotides, 20
nucleus, 16, 18

O
organelles, 12, 18, 20, 21, 22, 25, 26, 28, 31, 40

P
passive transport, 9
phospholipids, 7–9
photosynthesis, 27–28
primordial soup theory, 4–6

proteins, 12–13, 16, 21,
    22–23, 29, 31, 35
  fibrous, 13–14, 15
  globular, 15
  synthesis of, 18–20, 21,
    27, 36

R
red blood cells, 25, 40
ribosomes, 18–19, 20, 21, 22,
    31, 35
RNA (ribonucleic acid), 18, 19

S
secretory cells, 40
specialized cells,
    36–40

T
transfer RNA, 19, 20

W
white blood cells,
    24, 25

About the Author

Jennifer Viegas is a reporter for Discovery News, the news service for the Discovery Channel, and the Australian Broadcasting Corporation. She is a contributor to *New Scientist* and several other science magazines.

Credits

Cover © P. Motta & T. Naguto/Photo Researchers, Inc; pp. 5, 8, 10, 11, 17, 22, 24, 28, 30, 33 by Tahara Anderson; p. 6 © Alan Sirulnikoff/Science Photo Library; p. 14 © David M. Philips/The Population Council/Photo Researchers, Inc.; pp. 19, 26 © 2000-2004 Custom Medical Stock Photo; p. 25 © David McCarthy/Photo Researchers, Inc.; p. 37 © Ray Simons/Photo Researchers, Inc.; p. 38 © Omikron/Photo Researchers, Inc.; p. 39 © Prof. P. Motta/Univ. "La Sapienza;" p. 40 © P.Motta/Photo Researchers, Inc.; p. 41 (left) © SPL/Photo Researchers, Inc.; p. 41 (right) © David M. Phillips/Photo Researchers, Inc.

Designer: Tahara Anderson; **Editor:** Joann Jovinelly